In My Classroom And In My Home

A Young Child's View Of Montessori

by Katy Van Pelt

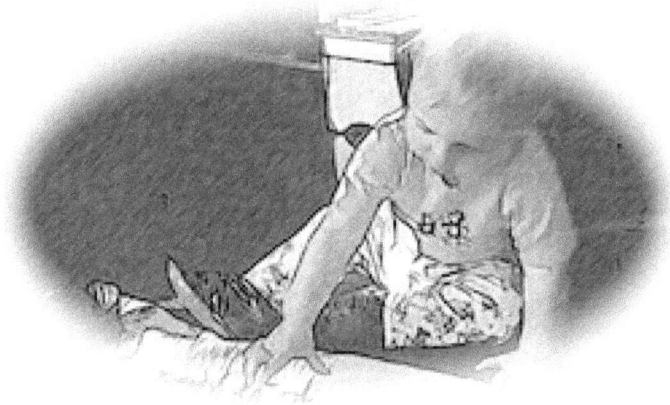

Blanket Press
www.blanketpressbooks.com
759 Rockland Avenue, Lake Bluff, Illinois 60044
Copyright © 2011 by Katy Van Pelt
All rights reserved, including the right of
reproduction in whole or in part.
Printed in the United States
ISBN 10: 0983300038
ISBN 13: 9780983300038

To Macsen, my youngest Montessori child

~~~

Special thanks to Forest Bluff Montessori School

In my classroom and in my home…

I have interesting work to do, and so I am interested in doing it.

In my classroom and in my
home…

I am surrounded by beauty,
and so I do beautiful work.

In my classroom and in my home…

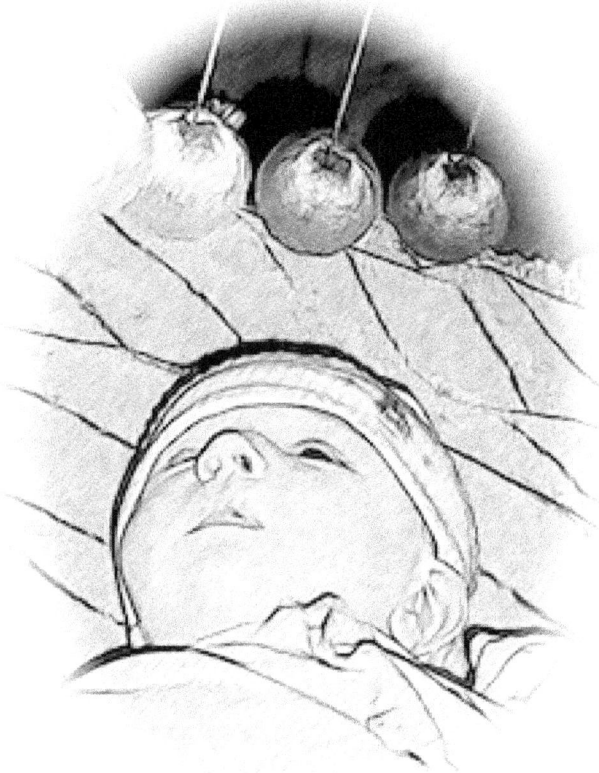

I have very important work to do, and so I feel important.

In my classroom and in my home...

My materials are precise,
and so I learn to work with
precision.

In my classroom and in my
home…

I have peaceful
surroundings, and so I learn
to concentrate with my
body and my mind.

In my classroom and in my home…

My work is real, and so I
learn to work with care and
thoughtfulness.

In my classroom and in my home...

My younger friends look to me for guidance, and so I help them to understand.

In my classroom and in my home…

I learn from books, and so I read them every day with others…

…and by myself.

In my classroom and in my home…

I help to prepare the meals…

…and so I enjoy eating
them.

In my classroom and in my home…

I learn about the world, and so I know that I am an important part of it.

In my classroom and in my home…

Others trust me, and so I
learn to trust myself.

In my classroom and in my
home…

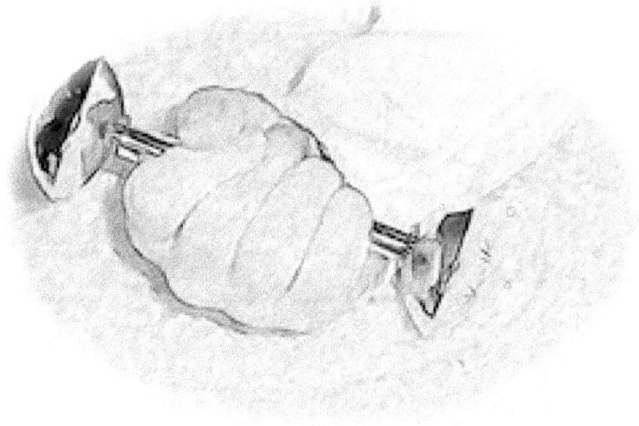

I have special objects to use,
and so I feel special when I
use them.

In my classroom and in my home…

People depend on me to do my work, and so I work hard to do it well.

In my classroom and in my home…

I try to find ways to make the environment more beautiful for everyone around me.

In my classroom and in my home…

Others believe in me, and so
I believe in myself.

In my classroom and in my
home…

I find joy in the natural
world around me.

In my classroom and in my
home…

I have jobs to do, and so I
feel needed.

In my classroom and in my home…

I am loved, and so I learn to love others.

In my classroom and in my home…

I am taken care of, and so I learn to take care of myself.

In my classroom and in my home…

I am important.

www.ingramcontent.com/pod-product-compliance
Lightning Source LLC
Chambersburg PA
CBHW060608030426
42337CB00019B/3665